THIS IS WHAT I PRAY TODAY

The Divine Hours™ Prayers for Children

PHYLLIS TICKLE

illustrated by

ELSA WARNICK

DUTTON CHILDREN'S BOOKS

DUTTON CHILDREN'S BOOKS

A division of Penguin Young Readers Group

Published by the Penguin Group • Penguin Group (USA) Inc.,

375 Hudson Street, New York, New York 10014, U.S.A.

Penguin Group (Canada), 90 Eglinton Avenue East, Suite 700, Toronto, Ontario, Canada M4P 2Y3

(a division of Pearson Penguin Canada Inc.) • Penguin Books Ltd, 80 Strand, London WC2R 0RL, England •

Penguin Ireland, 25 St Stephen's Green, Dublin 2, Ireland (a division of Penguin Books Ltd) •

Penguin Group (Australia), 250 Camberwell Road, Camberwell, Victoria 3124, Australia (a division of Pearson Australia

Group Pty Ltd) • Penguin Books India Pvt Ltd, 11 Community Centre, Panchsheel Park, New Delhi - 110 017, India •

Penguin Group (NZ), 67 Apollo Drive, Rosedale, North Shore 0745, Auckland,

New Zealand (a division of Pearson New Zealand Ltd) • Penguin Books (South Africa) (Pty) Ltd,

24 Sturdee Avenue, Rosebank, Johannesburg 2196, South Africa

Penguin Books Ltd, Registered Offices: 80 Strand, London WC2R 0RL, England

The Divine Hours™ Tickle, Inc.

CIP Data is available.

Published in the United States by Dutton Children's Books,

a division of Penguin Young Readers Group

345 Hudson Street, New York, New York 10014

www.penguin.com/youngreaders

Designed by IRENE VANDERVOORT

Manufactured in China

First Edition

ISBN 978-0-525-47828-7

1 3 5 7 9 10 8 6 4 2

$\mathcal{T}$hree times each day,
Little children like to pray:

It is God we thank for the morning sun
And for a brand-new day that has come.

Before we take our midday rest,
It is God's most holy name we bless.

And when the long, long day is done
And before the starry night has come,
It is God we ask to take our hand
And guide us gently into slumber land.

Sunday

WAKING UP

God hears me when I pray.
I know that this is so.
And I am going to speak to God today
In all the places where I go.

BASED ON PSALM 116:1–2

When I walk,
God walks with me.

When I run,
God runs with me.

When I talk,
God talks with me.

And when each day
Is almost done,
God stops a while
And rests with me.

BASED ON PSALM 139:7–10

ENDING MY DAY

*I*t's time to say good night, dear God,

To all the houses and the shops.

Good night to all the trucks and cars

That honk and wheeze, and stop and start.

It's time to say good night, dear God,

To all the friends I saw today.

Good night to the flowers and the trees,

To all the kittens and the puppies with their fleas.

It's time to say good night, dear God,

And thank You for these lovely things.

BASED ON PSALM 4:7–8

Monday

WAKING UP

Keep my little feet, Lord,
Everywhere they walk today.

Keep my little hands, Lord,
Everywhere they play today.

Keep my little eyes, Lord,
Everywhere they look today.

Keep my little soul, Lord,
Everywhere we go today.

BASED ON PSALM 116:8–9

RESTING

God is the sky,
Bright and blue,
Up above me high.

God is the earth
Beneath my happy feet,
Warm and soft and dry.

God is the air
Between them both,
Sweet and clean and near.

There God always sees
And ever keeps me
In gentle love and care.

BASED ON PSALM 115:16

ENDING MY DAY

*G*od made the darkness.

God made the light.

God made them both alike.

God loves the darkness.

God loves the light.

God loves them both alike.

God blesses the darkness.

God blesses the light.

God blesses them both alike.

Please, God, bless me in the darkness.

Please, God, bless me in the light.

Please, God, bless me in them both alike.

BASED ON PSALM 139:11–12

Tuesday

WAKING UP

Thank You, God, for the fields,

For flowers that bloom and bees that buzz.

Thank You, God, for the sun and sky,

For clouds that drift and birds that fly.

Thank You, God, for the woods and trees,

For squirrels that scurry and turtles that sun.

Thank You for all these happy things I see,

And thank You most of all for making me.

BASED ON PSALM 89:15&18

RESTING

God loves the flowers.
God loves the trees.
God loves me.

I love flowers.
I love trees.
And I love God,
Just as God loves me.

BASED ON PSALM 139:14–16

ENDING MY DAY

Outside my window there are rustling trees
And, in my curtains, a little breeze.
Hush, hush. Sing lullaby.

Inside my house there are grown-ups near,
Who smile and hug and call me dear.
Hush, hush. Sing lullaby.

Outside my window the sun is almost gone.
Inside my house the lights are coming on.
Hush, hush. Sing lullaby.

Inside my house and very near,
Someone smiles and whispers, "God is here."
Hush, hush. Sing lullaby.

BASED ON PSALM 134

Wednesday

WAKING UP

*F*or stores and clouds and trees,

For cats and cars and bumblebees,

Thank You, God.

For books and coats and toys,

And for other little girls and boys,

Thank You, God.

For dogs and horns and keys,

For food and fun and scuffed-up knees,

Thank You, God, for everything.

BASED ON PSALM 86:4–5

RESTING

*M*y day is halfway done,
And the sun's is, too.
But before I take a little rest,
I want to speak to You.

What I pray, dear Lord,
Is that someday very soon
I can be like a little sun
And shine all day for You.

BASED ON PSALM 19:2–6

ENDING MY DAY

God is outside me,
God is inside me,
God is all around me,
All through the day.

But now the day is done,
And this is what I pray:

God, be above me;
God, be below me;
God, please watch beside me,
Until there is another day.

BASED ON PSALM 72:17

Thursday

WAKING UP

$\mathcal{T}$each me to be kind today,

The way You are kind to me.

Teach me to see my friends today,

The way You see me.

Teach me to love everyone I meet today,

Just the way, dear God, that You love me.

BASED ON PSALM 86:4–5

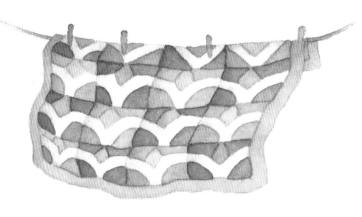

RESTING

*T*hank you, God,

for watching over me.

Thank you, God,

for taking care of me.

Thank you, God,

for always loving me.

Thank you, God,

for angels who will rest with me.

BASED ON PSALM 91:11–13

ENDING MY DAY

*T*hank You for my warm bed.
Thank You for the pillow
Beneath my sleepy head.

Thank You for the dark tonight.
Thank You for tomorrow
And another morning's light.

BASED ON PSALM 121:5–7

Friday

WAKING UP

God made this day for me.
God made this world for me.
God made lots of words for me.

I thank You, God, for Your day.
I thank You, God, for Your world.
And help me thank You, God,
With all the words I say.

BASED ON PSALM 118:24

RESTING

Dear God, I know You made the seas,

The tides, and all the ships that sail upon them.

I know you make the waves, dear Lord,

And every sandy beach that holds them.

So what I pray just now, dear Lord,

Is that You'll hold and cuddle me

Just the way You hold and rock the sea.

BASED ON PSALM 93

ENDING MY DAY

*D*ear God, three things I want to know before I go to bed:

Will You smile at me in my dreams tonight?

In the darkness, will You be my light?

And will You keep me always in Your sight

While I am asleep tonight?

Dear God, three things I'm glad I know before I go to bed:

You will smile at me in my dreams tonight;

In the darkness, You will be my light;

And You will keep me always in Your sight

While I am asleep tonight.

BASED ON PSALM 4:6–8

Saturday

WAKING UP

With my eyes I see.

With my ears I hear.

With my arms I hug.

With my heart I love.

God, bless everyone I see today.

God, bless everyone I hear today.

God, bless everyone I hug today.

God, bless everyone I love today.

This is what I pray today.

BASED ON PSALM 63:3–5

RESTING

y little legs are tired.
My little eyes are, too.

When we stop to rest a while,

I think that God rests, too.

BASED ON PSALM 3:5

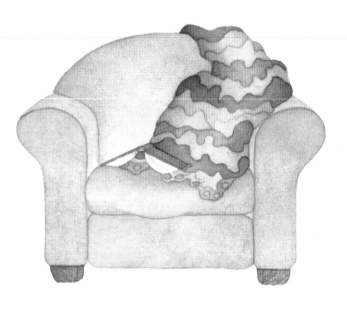

ENDING MY DAY

*I*t's time to stop my play.

It's time to end my day.

Now I have my prayers to say:

God, hold me tight tonight.

God, keep me safe tonight.

God, bless us every one

All through the night.

BASED ON PSALM 140:12–13; 141:1–2

$\mathcal{T}$eaching our older children and young adults to pray at set times each day has always been a part of religious instruction for the world's great monotheistic faiths of Judaism, Christianity, and Islam. This small prayer book, however, is for a much younger audience.

While this volume will certainly function as simply a book of prayers for young children, it is intended primarily to be a "prayer book." That is, *This Is What I Pray Today* offers Christian, Jewish, and Muslim parents and grand-parents a means by which the very young can be introduced early to the patterns and very grown-up practice of fixed-hour prayer. Just as importantly, this volume gives little ones a first prayer book of their very own to treasure, one by means of which they too, from time to time, can even participate in the company of the adults around them who pray the hours.

Time is a gift from God and a holy thing. By marking it at regular intervals each day with our prayers of thanks-giving, and by teaching our children to do so, we honor both the role of time in ordering our lives and the greatness of the gift God has given in creating it for us. None of us are too young to rejoice in that.

PHYLLIS TICKLE